© Copyright 2020 - All rights reserved.

The content contained within this book may not be reproduced, duplicated or transmitted without direct written permission from the author or the publisher. Under no circumstances will any blame or legal responsibility be held against the publisher, or author, for any damages, reparation, or monetary loss due to the information contained within this book, either directly or indirectly.

Legal Notice:

This book is copyright protected. It is only for personal use. You cannot amend, distribute, sell, use, quote or paraphrase any part, or the content within this book, without the consent of the author or publisher.

Disclaimer Notice:

Please note the information contained within this document is for educational and entertainment purposes only. All effort has been executed to present accurate, up to date, reliable, complete information. No warranties of any kind are declared or implied. Readers acknowledge that the author is not engaged in the rendering of legal, financial, medical or professional advice. The content within this book has been derived from various sources.

Please consult a licensed professional before attempting any techniques outlined in this book. By reading this document, the reader agrees that under no circumstances is the author responsible for any losses, direct or indirect, that are incurred as a result of the use of the information contained within this document, including,but not limited to, errors, omissions, or inaccuracies.

INTRODUCTION

It is recognized that coloring activity has great virtues in our behavior and on the brain. Indeed, coloring will allow you to isolate yourself, to cut you off from the world for a pencil stroke. This is why many people call these drawings anti-stress coloring. In addition, the advantage of these colorings, is of course the possibility to remake them to infinity with new color palettes, and thus give them a whole other aspect. Hours of fun and relaxation to color these coloring pages for both kids and adults!

This coloring activity book may assist you in achieving following health benefits

REDUCE STRESS AND ANXIETY
Coloring induces the same state as meditating by reducing the thoughts of a restless mind. This generates mindfulness and quietness, which allows your mind to get some rest after a long day at work.

IMPROVE MOTOR SKILLS AND VISION
Coloring requires the two hemispheres of the brain to communicate. While logic helps us stay inside the lines, choosing colors generates a creative thought process.

IMPROVE SLEEP
Coloring is a relaxing and electronic-free bedtime ritual that won't disturb your level of melatonin.

IMPROVE FOCUS
Coloring requires you to focus, but not so much that it's stressful. It opens up your frontal lobe, which controls organizing and problem solving, and allows you to put everything else aside and live in the moment, generating focus.

Source : www.beaumont.org

It's time to warm up and get your creative juices flowing
This shape is called mandala which has been used through-out the history in a spiritual sense
Try different color schemes and see how it turns out in the end

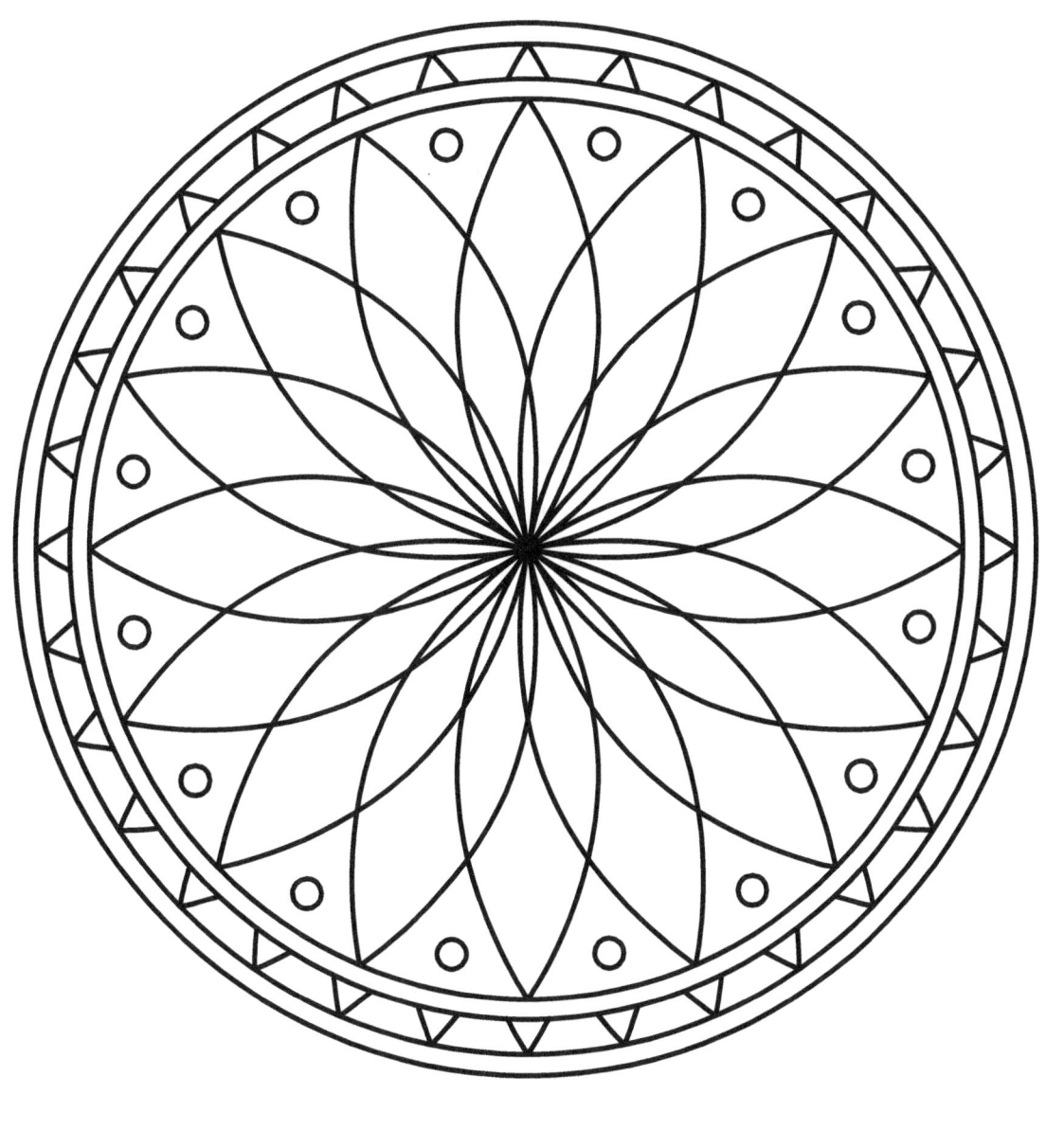

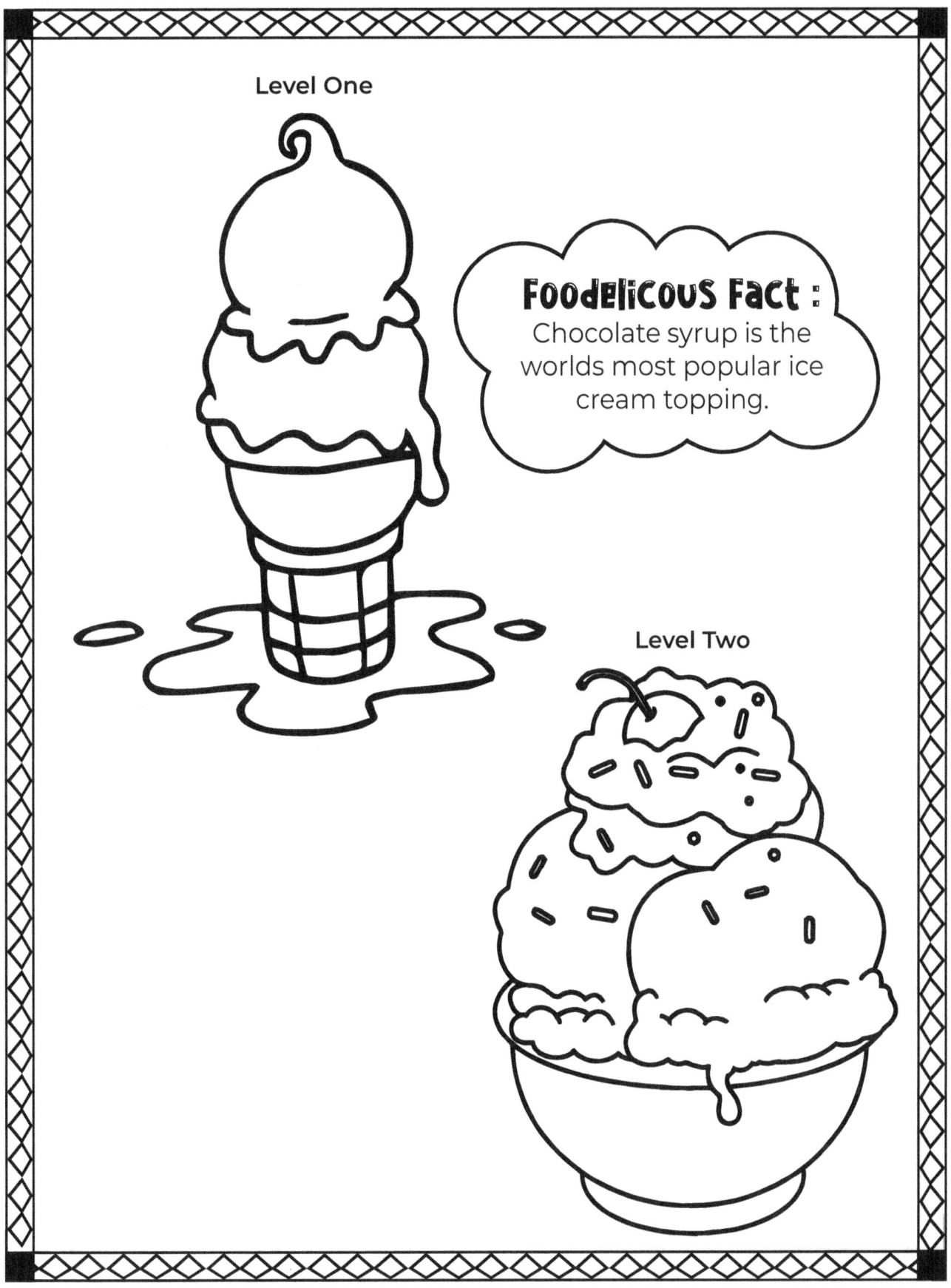

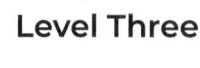

Level Three

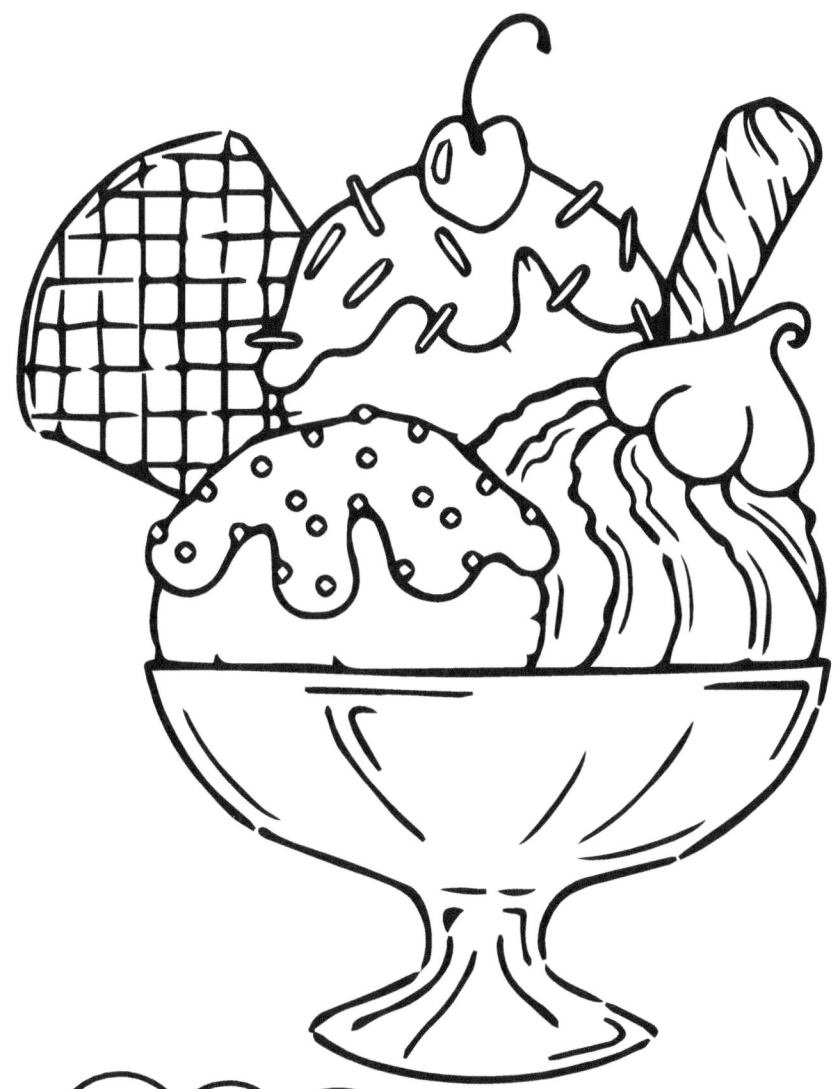

Foodelicous Fact:
87% of Americans have ice-cream in their freezers at any given time

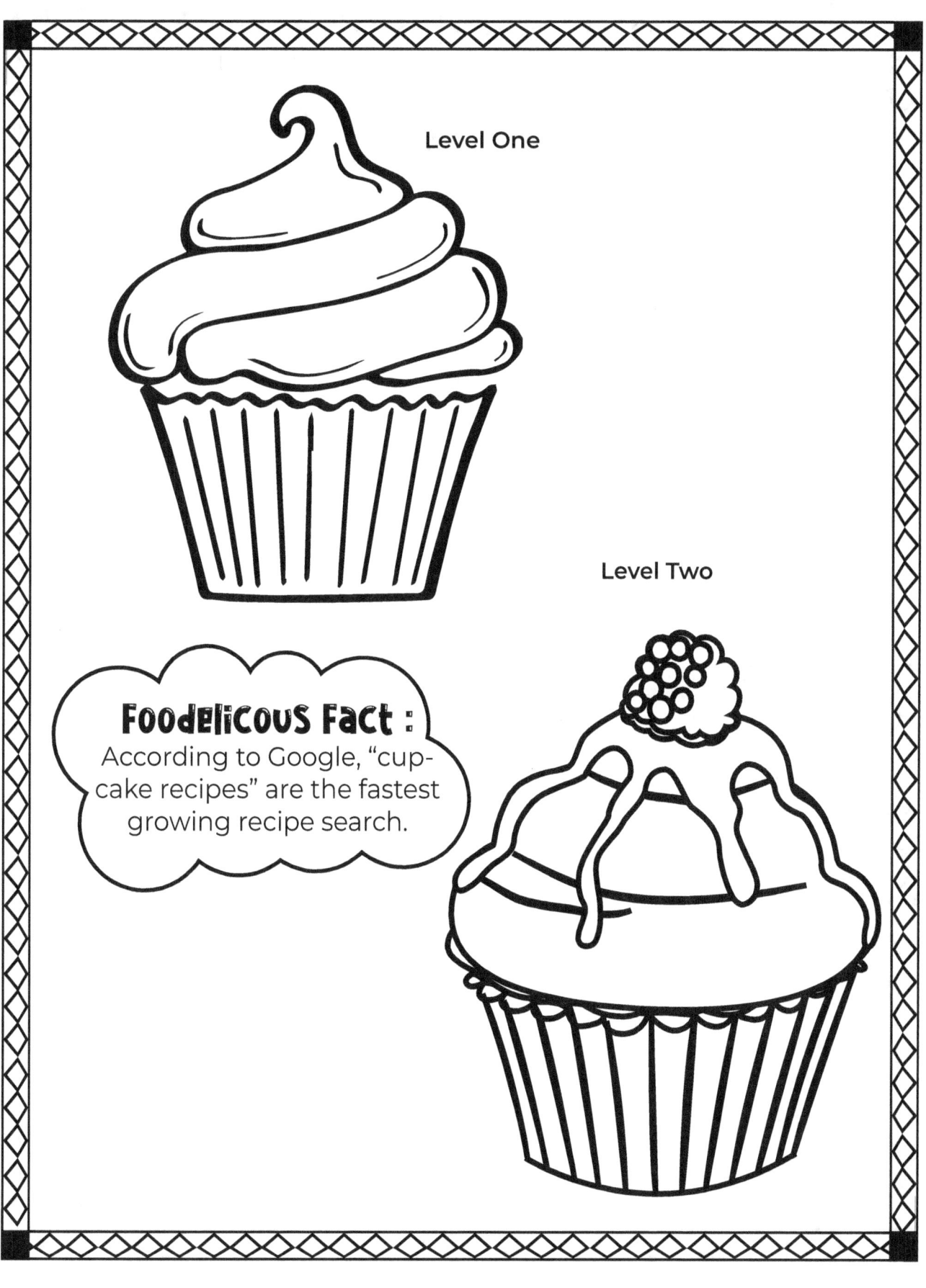

Level Three

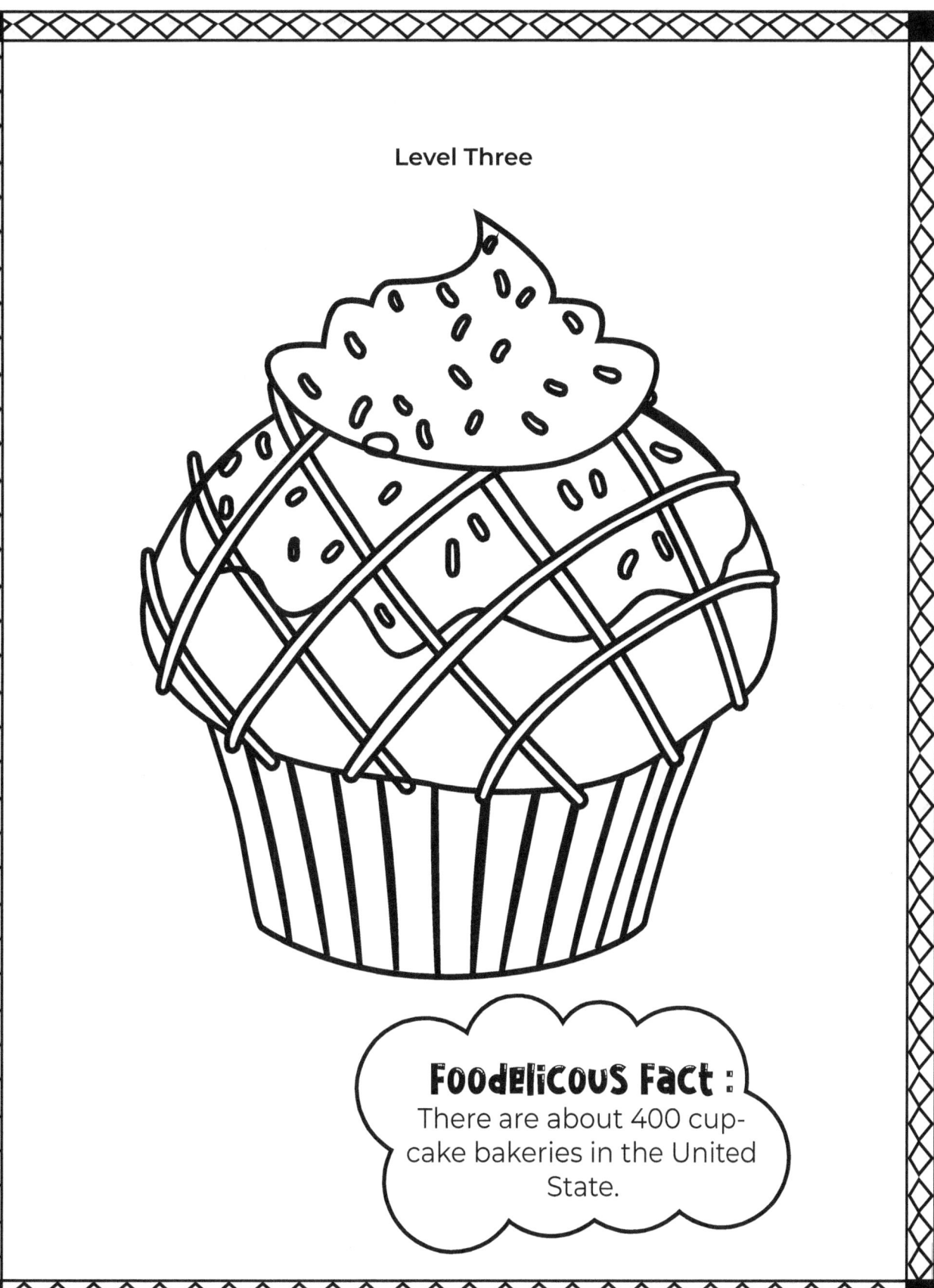

Foodelicous Fact:
There are about 400 cupcake bakeries in the United State.

Level Three

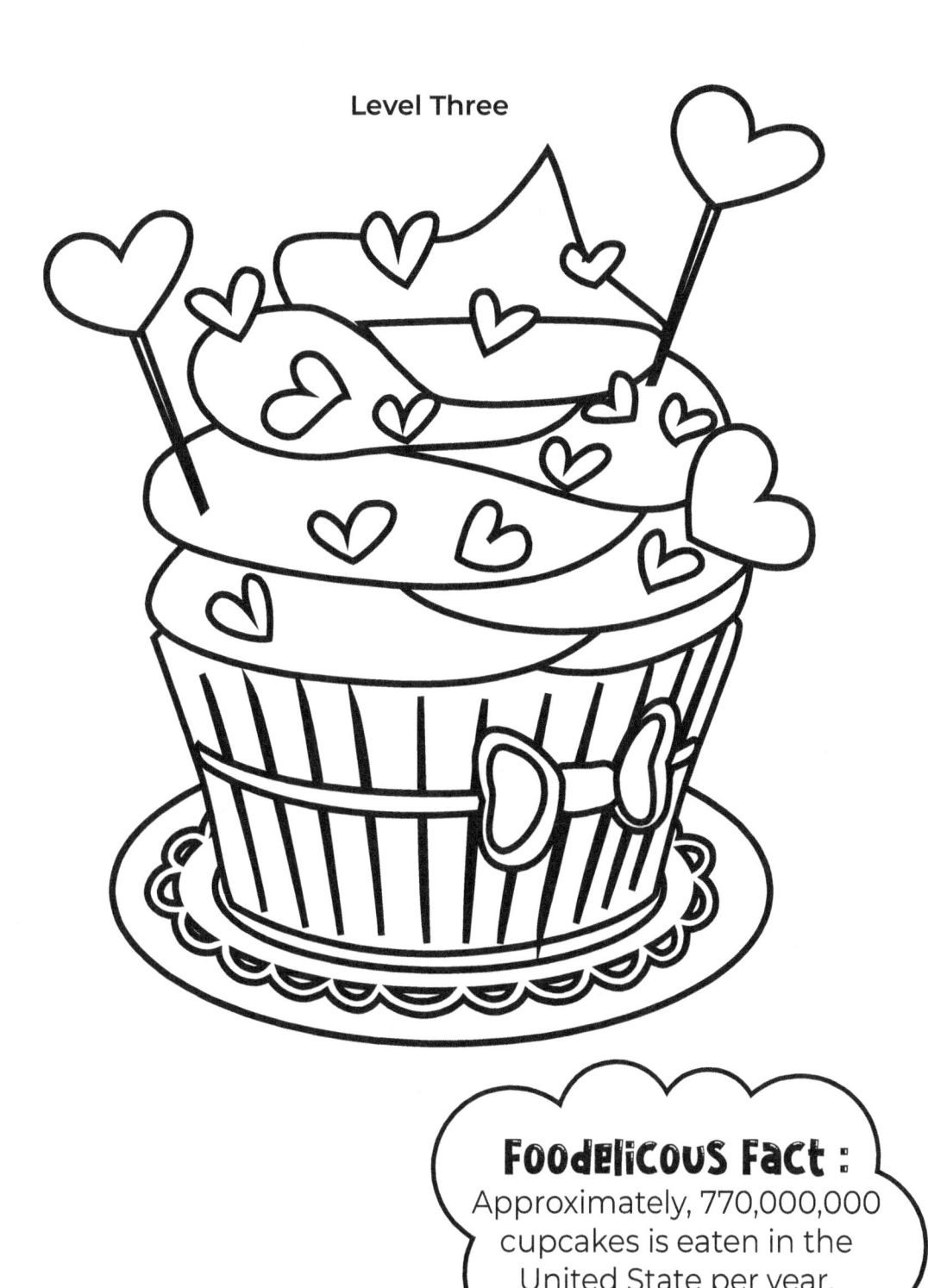

Foodelicous Fact:
Approximately, 770,000,000 cupcakes is eaten in the United State per year.

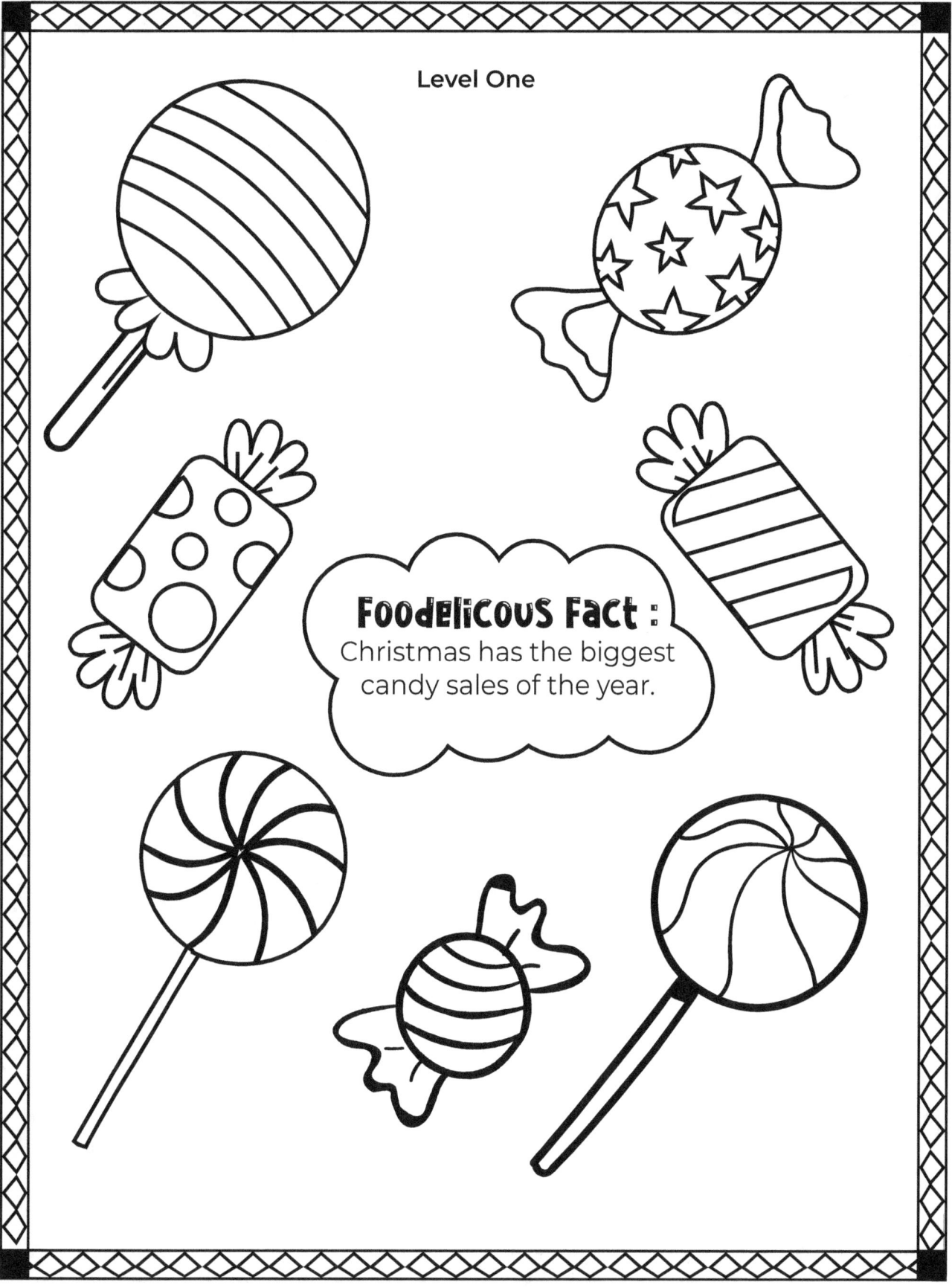

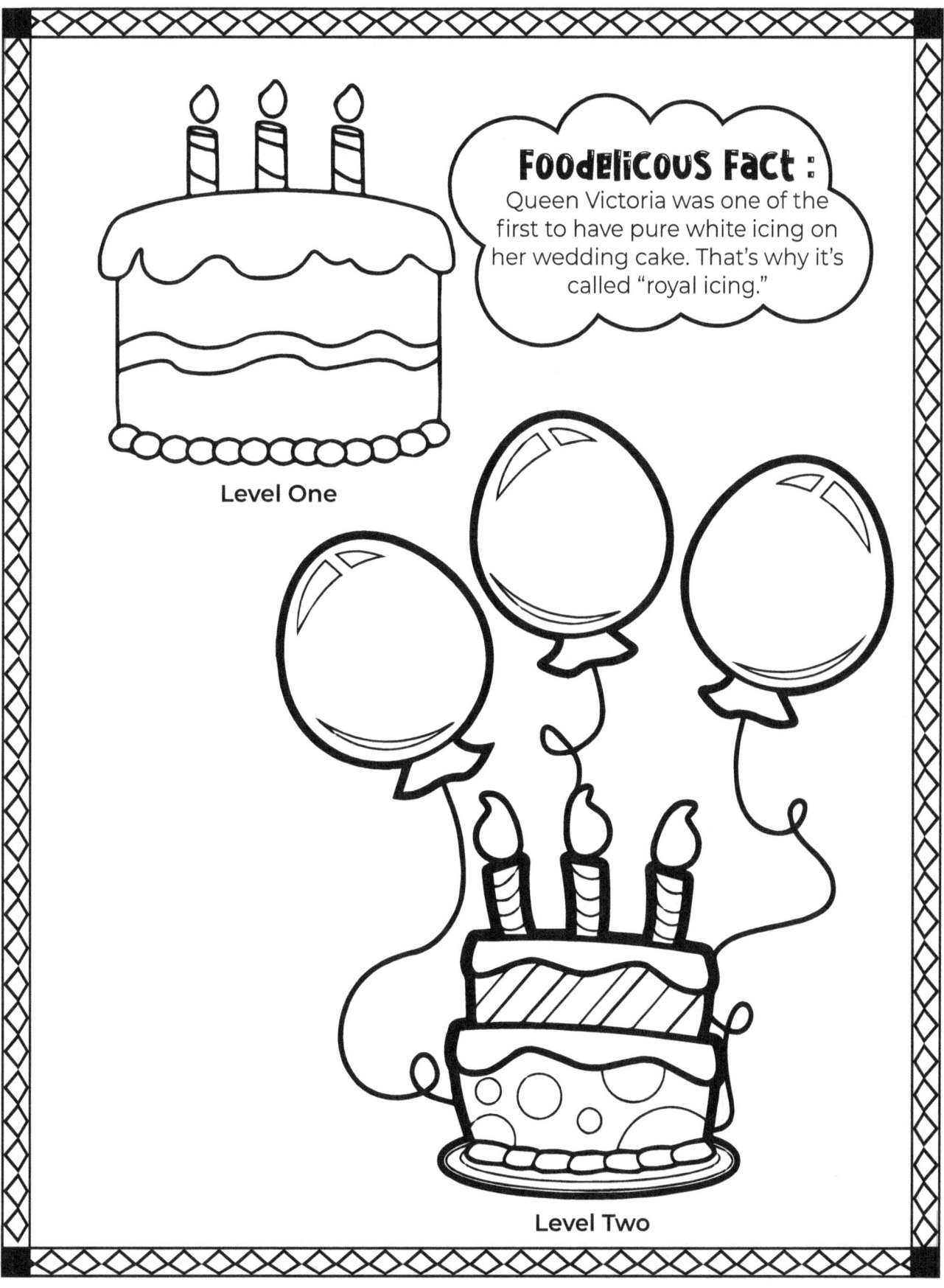

Level One

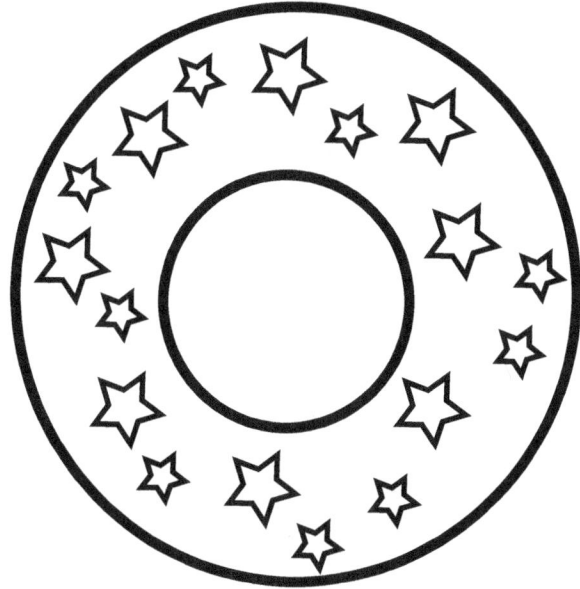

Foodelicous Fact:
THERE ARE 10 PEOPLE LIVING IN AMERICA WITH THE LAST NAME "DOUGHNUT" OR "DONUT."

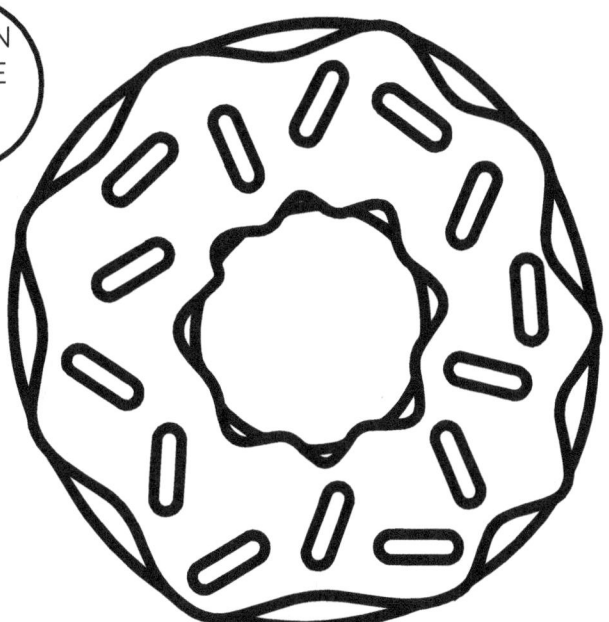

Level Two

Level Three

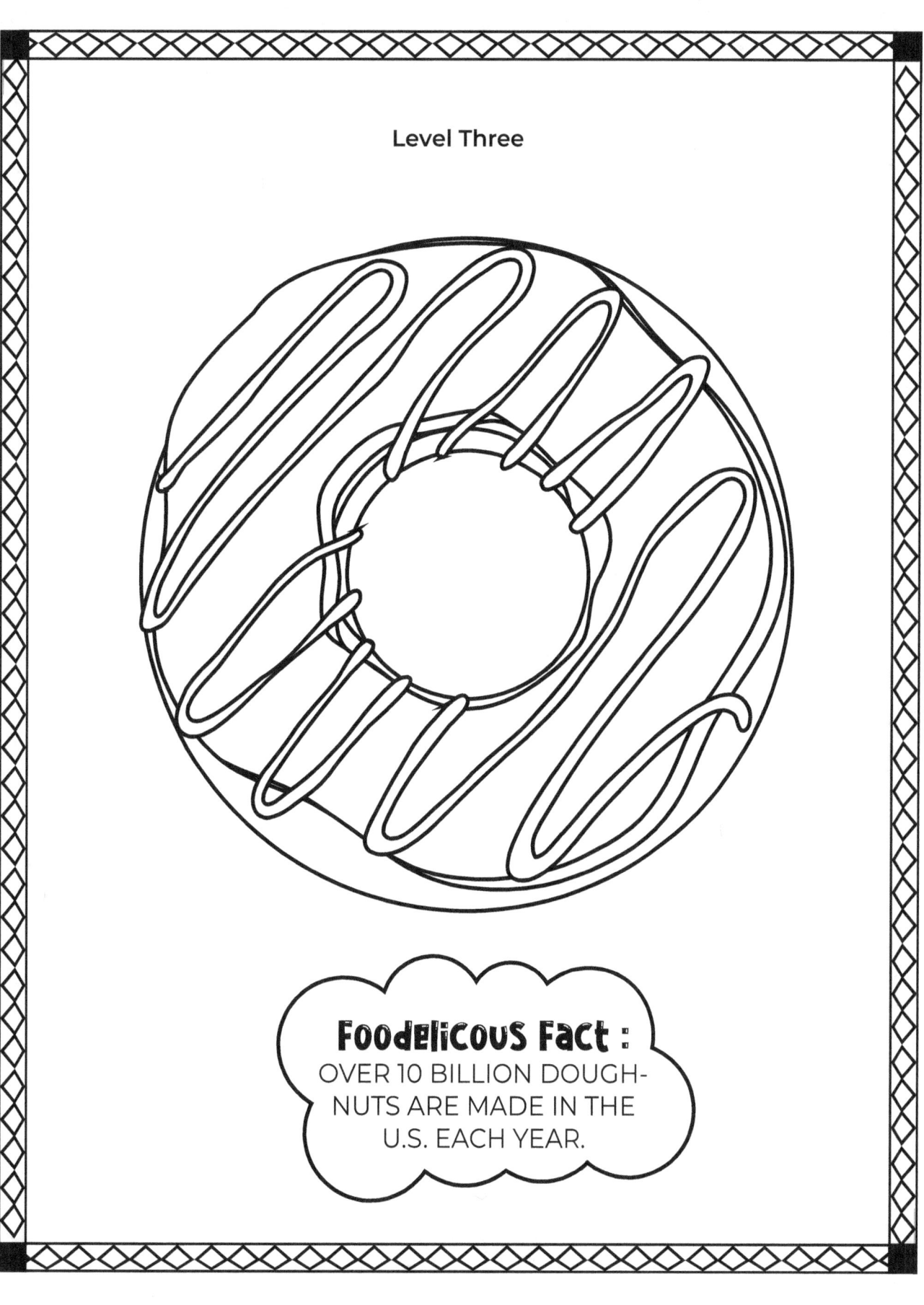

Foodelicious Fact:
OVER 10 BILLION DOUGH-
NUTS ARE MADE IN THE
U.S. EACH YEAR.

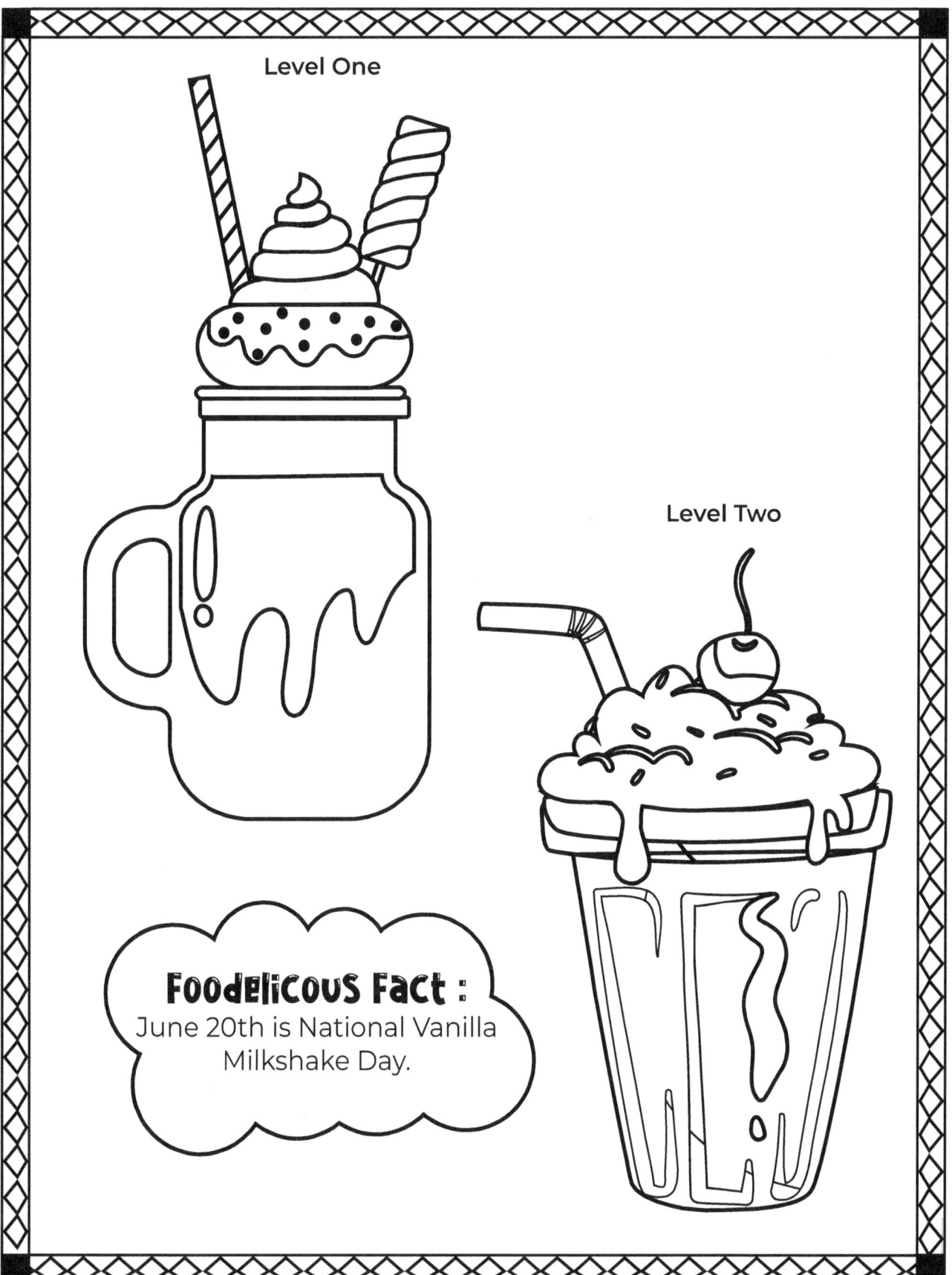

Level Three

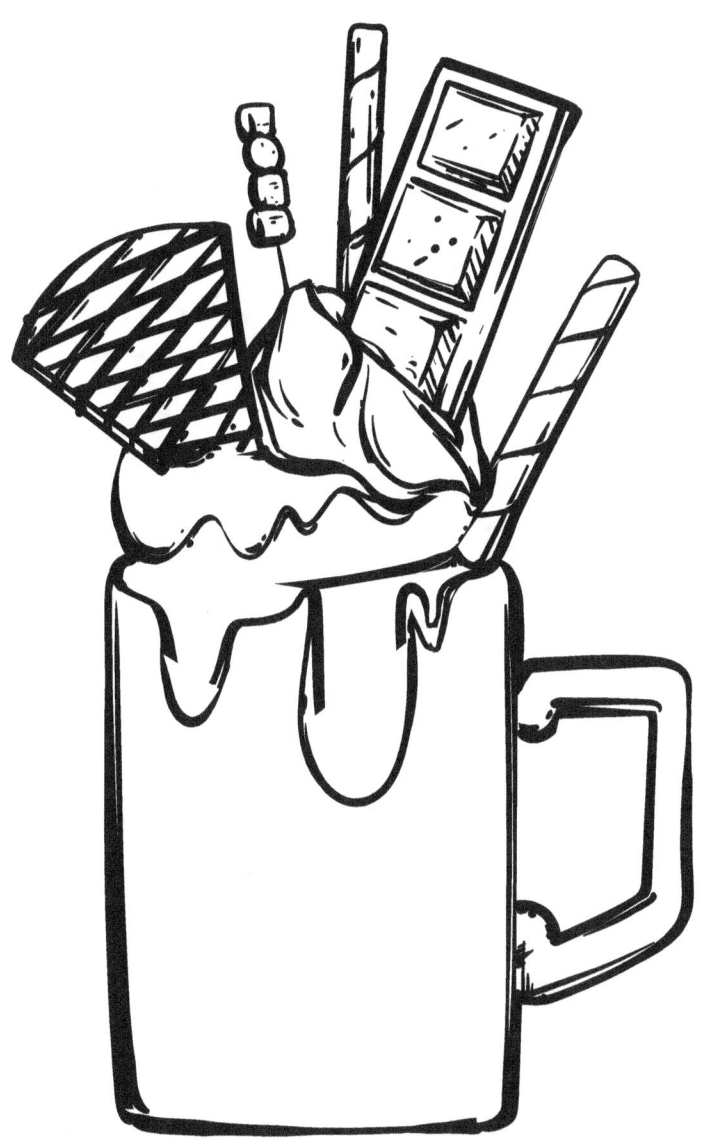

Foodelicous Fact :
September 12th is National Chocolate Milkshake Day.

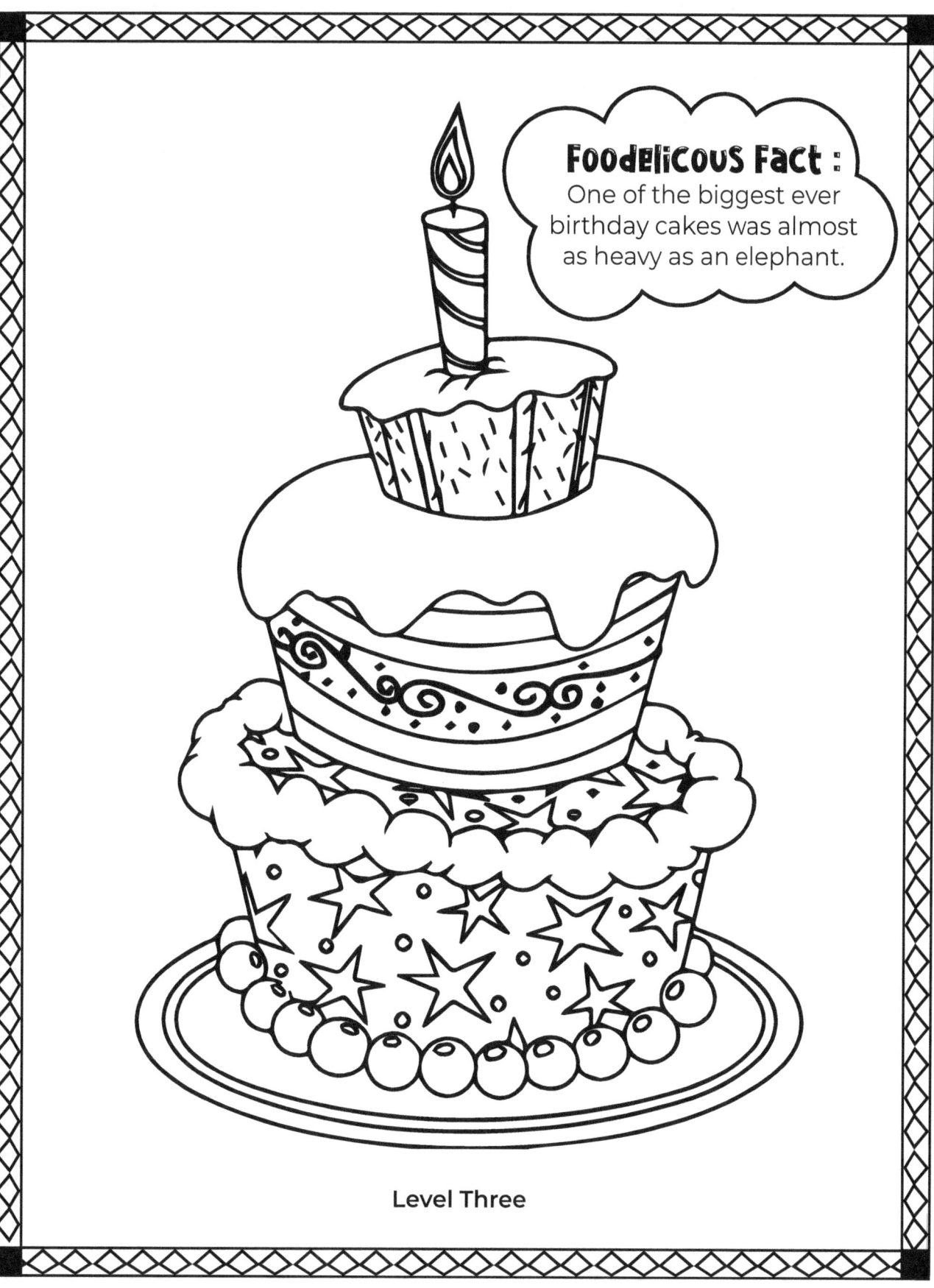

START HERE

Can you reach your cupcake within 12 seconds?

Ending Note

We hope that your journey with our book was delicious , We would love to hear your feedback so we can improve this journey next time
We would be grateful if you leave a short review on Amazon
Your appreciation will be a great motivation for us

For any other queries please feel free to email us
meroxkhan@gmail.com

www.ingramcontent.com/pod-product-compliance
Lightning Source LLC
Chambersburg PA
CBHW081100240526
45465CB00025B/2792